FIXED INCOME INSIGHTS OF A BOND MAN

Mark J. Angioletti

Table of Contents

Disclaimer

The opinions expressed in this book are solely those of the author. No part of this book is to be construed as specific individual investment advice. The author of this book is not responsible or liable for any investment losses incurred by individuals attempting to follow strategies provided in this book. Investors should always consult with an experienced registered financial adviser before investing.

Dedication

This book is dedicated to investors looking to simplify investment strategy.

Introduction

What justifies a book discussing fixed income securities in an environment of vanishingly low interest rates? Successful investing like any endeavor depends on information: My forty-years of Financial Services Industry experience has demonstrated investors not fortunate enough to inherit oil wells, timberland, mines, or income producing real estate invest in publicly traded securities; often without even a rudimentary knowledge of the securities they're investing in. The U.S. capital markets transact billions of dollars of fixed income securities every day, yet few investors understand this sector of the capital markets.

The opaque pricing structure and confusing terminology of fixed income markets persuades most investors to opt for readily available derivative products (mutual funds, CEFs, ETFs, UITs, etc.) the Financial Services Industry provides to simplify investing. In their quest to generate investment income, investors often overlook the high built in fee structure that forces fund managers to resort to the use of leverage[1] and lower rated securities to boost managed products' yield. Unfortunately, portfolio yield enhancement strategies can magnify price volatility and adversely impact shareholders' capital.

Like most developed nations[2], the United States faces a rapidly aging population that gravitates to income investments – failure to understand fixed income credit quality ratings misdirects many safety-oriented investors to view current yield or lack of price volatility as indicators of safety, rather than timely payment of interest and principal: a misunderstanding that can have disastrous results.

The financial media often denigrates the investment benefits of fixed income securities, expounding equities as the investments of choice, yet fixed income securities are the largest sector of the capital markets and Treasury securities[3] provide

---

1 Borrowed capital.

2 France, Germany, Great Britain, Japan etc.

3 Treasury securities are a non-correlated asset that appreciate in price (flight to quality) during equity market melt downs.

safety and liquidity during a financial market crisis.

Sincerely,

Mark J. Angioletti

Chapter 1: The Benchmark

On August 6th, 2011, Standard & Poor's Financial Services LLC citing increased concerns regarding the ballooning U.S. Government deficit and the U.S. Congress's lack of initiative to control the growing deficit made worldwide headlines by downgrading the credit rating of U.S. Treasury securities from "AAA" to "AA+": The two other major credit ratings agencies, Moody's and Fitch Investors Services, maintained the U.S. Treasury's "AAA" rating.

With over $17 trillion outstanding, U.S. Treasury securities comprise the largest most liquid securities market in the world. Backed by the Full Faith and Credit of the United States Treasury, investors buy Treasury securities for safety of principal and income. Standard & Poor's strong message regarding Congress's laxed resolve in dealing with the Federal budget did not significantly impact the pricing of U.S. Treasuries across the yield curve[4].

---

4 A yield curve plots the yields of fixed income securities vs. their respective maturities.

The size and liquidity of the U.S. Treasury market facilitates pricing of all other fixed income securities: The Treasury yield curve is the benchmark which other fixed income securities are priced at a basis point spread[5] to the corresponding maturity Treasury security – price discovery is paramount to the proper functioning of securities markets.

Americans often forget the United States didn't begin life as a global superpower, as recently as the early 20th Century, the U.S. was an emerging market economy possessing a youthful population and vast resources. During the first decades of the 20th Century, America's untapped potential was safely isolated by two oceans and prudent U.S. Government budget control precluded the need for debt issuance until the Great Depression of the 1930's.

During the 1920's and '30s the largest corporation in the world, American Telephone & Telegraph (AT&T), held a "AAA" debt rating making its' debt securities the benchmark U.S. fixed income markets

---

5 Technically this is referred to as the credit spread because it differentiates yields across different levels of credit worthiness.

used to determine the yield spread on lower rated debt securities.

As the 1930's saw the U.S. economy mired in the Great Depression and U.S. industrial capacity utilization languished at 30%, the Federal Government under President Roosevelt's "New Deal" started running Federal budget deficits to counter the loss of private sector jobs with Federal Government funded make work programs. In 1935, President Roosevelt signed into law legislation creating Series A Savings Bonds to provide the U.S. Treasury funding for depression era programs.

Luckily, the U.S. had established a debt issuance program prior to December 7th, 1941. After the attack on the U.S. Naval installation at Pearl Harbor, the production of war materials expanded industrial capacity utilization to 100% which the U.S. Government financed by issuing War Bonds (renamed Savings Bonds).

Emerging from World War II with 50% of the global productive capacity, the United States proceeded to finance global infrastructure reconstruction via issuance of Treasury debt

– deficit spending that expanded the Treasury security market through the 1940's and '50s. Unfortunately, U.S. deficit spending continued through much of the '60s, '70s, '80s, '90s, and into the 21st Century causing the U.S. Treasury securities market to become the largest securities market in the world.

Many U.S. investors overlook the U.S. dollar ($) is the reserve currency of the globe; essential commodities such as corn, wheat, soybeans, oil, copper, gold etc., are quoted in dollars, the U.S. dollar is the transaction currency of global business. Foreign corporations often hold dollar denominated profits in U.S. Treasury securities, foreign governments hold dollar denominated reserves in U.S. Treasury securities, and foreign entities issue fixed income securities[6] denominated in dollars that are priced at a yield spread to the corresponding Treasury maturities to attract U.S. investors.

Currently, Treasury securities are held by U.S. domiciled entities; corporations, partnerships, banks, trusts, etc.; U.S.

---

6 Sovereign and Corporate

citizens, foreign governments, and foreign corporations – making U.S. Treasury securities the most widely distributed securities in the world.

Capital markets utilize Treasury securities maturity designation terminology: bills (securities shorter than one year sold at a discount to par value[7]), notes (coupon bearing securities with maturities of one to ten years), and bonds (securities longer than ten years[8]) for all fixed income securities – while the financial media often refers to all but the shortest fixed income securities as bonds, a misleading simplification.

Frequently the financial media discusses the current Fed Funds rate without mentioning its' relationship to the Treasury yield curve: The Fed Funds rate is the designated interest rate range at which depository institutions can lend overnight trade balances held at the Federal Reserve, making it the shortest maturity for which interest is accrued and the only rate the Federal Reserve officially controls.

---

7 Par value or Face value for a standard bond is $1000 and is quoted in bond terminology as 100.

8 B-N-B, Bills, Notes, Bonds

The U.S. Treasury currently issues 1-mo., 2-mo., 3-mo., 6-mo., and 1-yr. bills; 2-yr., 3-yr., 5-yr., 7-yr., and 10-yr. notes; along with 20-yr. and 30-yr. bonds, Series EE savings bonds, zero coupon STRIPS[9] with maturities out to 30-years, and for investors seeking inflation adjusted returns Treasury TIPS (Treasury Inflation Protected Securities) in 5-yr., 10-yr., and 20-yr. maturities.

Fixed income maturity nomenclature is relatively easy to grasp, but the inverse relationship between price and yield causes confusion for many investors. Fixed income security prices are quoted as a percentage of par (100) with the current yield and the yield to maturity stated as a one-year percentage of face value. Appendix 1 provides a formula to calculate yield to maturity from three variables (coupon, price, and time to maturity).

Understanding the impact of interest rate changes on fixed income security pricing can be illustrated with a simple example: a

---

9 Separate Trading of Registered Interest and Principal of Securities.

hypothetical 10% coupon 10-yr. Treasury note currently priced at par paying $100 yearly interest will rise in price approximately $100 for a 100 basis points (1%) downward move in interest rates to yield 9% – the rough[10] yield calculation is as follows, $100 (yearly Interest payment) / price = 9% or approximately 110 (bond parlance for $1,100)[11]. Conversely, if interest rates were to rise 100 basis points, a 10% coupon 10-yr. Treasury note currently priced at par would fall in price approximately $90 ($100/ 910 = 11%) – the fixed coupon forces the markets' current yield to be reflected in the price.

The example used the same basis point change in interest rates (100 points down and 100 points up) to demonstrate a fixed income security's price sensitivity to a one hundred basis point change in interest rates. While the 10% coupon Treasury security rose approximately 10% in price for a 100-basis point downward move in rates, it dropped by 9.1% for a 10% upward move in

---

10 This is a raw current yield calculation for illustrative purposes, not a yield to maturity.

11 This comparison uses Treasury note yields, only coupon and maturity are variables, credit quality remains the same.

rates, a difference is due to a combination of yield calculation[12] and the effect of duration.

Duration[13] is security market terminology for time weighted average of cash flows accruing to a security – Modified duration is a measure of a fixed income security's price sensitivity to interest rate change. High coupons[14] have lower sensitivity to interest rate changes due to the reinvestment of the larger coupon amount: The higher the current cash flow, the shorter the time horizon for a security's price change to offset an interest rate rise, hence higher coupon securities have a shorter duration and exhibit lower price volatility. The shorter duration of high coupon securities is an important reason portfolio manager buy premium priced[15] (par+) vs. discount priced (less than par) securities. Unfortunately, until an interest rate rise decimates the market value of their fixed income portfolio most investors gravitate to discount priced

---

12 See Appendix 1 for an explanation of calculating yield to maturity.

13 Macaulay Duration

14 Assuming all other factors i.e. maturity, quality and fixed income sector are the same.

15 Lower price volatility during rising interest rates.

securities rather than premium priced securities.

While the discussion has centered on Treasury securities, duration applies to all fixed income instruments. Higher coupon securities of similar quality rating always provide shorter duration and lower price volatility when compared to similar quality rated lower coupon securities. Zero-coupon bonds, the lowest of all coupons, have the highest price volatility for any maturity of similar quality rating: The duration of a zero-coupon bond always matches its maturity date.[16]

The relationship of duration and maturity highlights a strategy many investors fail to exploit. The Treasury market typically exhibits a normal shaped yield curve: yield vs. maturity plotted horizontally is upward sloping to the right with yields increasing as maturity extends. With a normal shaped yield curve, 5 to 7-yr. Treasury notes typically yield 95% of the yield of longer-term maturities (20 to 30-yrs.). Rising yields across the normal Treasury yield curve

---

16 "Zeros" provide no coupon interest to reinvest.

provides holders of 5 to 7-yr. Treasury securities the benefit of an appealing yield combined with a shorter maturity's lower price volatility[17]. The erosion of time continuously shortens the maturities of all fixed income securities, after two-years a 5-yr. note becomes a 3-yr. note , a 7-yr. note becomes a 5-yr. note etc.: Investment professionals refer to the erosion of maturity as "rolling down the yield curve" [18]. Time erosion shortens the maturity of the higher coupon notes allowing their price to trade at a premium to a lower coupon corresponding maturity issue, often providing holders of the reduced maturity note an opportunity to sell at a higher price than they originally paid. Due to the mistaken belief they can accurately predict interest rate changes, investors fearing an interest rate rise, prefer to own short maturity fixed income securities – with a normal shaped Treasury yield curve an investor can often buy securities with a longer time horizon, receive a higher current yield, and sell at a favorable price if liquidity is required. Unfortunately, most investors

---

17 Similar coupon shorter maturity provides lower duration hence lower volatility.
18 This is real bond market terminology.

forfeit a higher current yield by buying shorter maturity securities that matches their target liquidity date in the belief that an interest rate rise will decimate the market price of their securities when they need to sell.

During the late 1970's the U.S. Treasury changed the issuance of its' longest maturity from 40-years to a 30-year non-callable security: from that time on all newly issued Treasury securities were non-callable. The Treasury's issuance policy was contrary to the policy of corporate and municipal debt issuers that believed interest rates would eventually reverse direction and didn't want to be locked into high coupon long-term debt without call provisions while buyers of new issue corporate and municipal debt wanted to lock in the high coupon payments long as possible: The trade-off issuers devised was the 10-year call provision, which most debt, except Treasury securities, are currently issued with.

While Treasury securities are the safest, most widely distributed security in the world, most investors are unaware the U.S. Treasury currently holds weekly auctions of varying size (depending on the Treasury's changing financing needs) that are posted on the Treasury's website. Currently, the average maturity of all outstanding Treasury debt is less than seven years, forcing Treasury auctions to facilitate rolling over of maturing debt along with accommodating any additional Treasury financing needs – the net effect is variation in the size and maturities of the auction schedule.

The size of the Treasury auction and the average accepted yield impacts secondary market pricing: If designated Treasury dealers end-up with excess inventory, secondary market prices will drop after the auction closes, making dealer bidding an important component of every Treasury auction.

Investors have the option of buying Treasury securities directly from the Treasury Direct website or from a financial services firm they use to execute equity trades. Purchasing Treasury securities through a financial services firm provides investors the convenience of consolidating their portfolio holdings in one account along with the possibility of utilizing same day settlement Treasury trades to resolve a short-term cash problem.

Investor' greed at market tops often increases equity market allocation beyond their designated target level – maintaining the appropriate portfolio allocation to Treasury securities or cash when equity markets appear poised to move higher can be emotionally difficult. Treasury securities are a non-correlated asset that will rise in price (flight to safety) during equity market panics. During the 2008 financial market crisis, only Treasury securities and cash provided protection from the financial slaughter. Investors holding cash or Treasury securities can benefit from investment opportunities provided by a market sell-off.

Chapter 2: Agencies of Opportunity

Chapter 1 described the $17 trillion U.S. Treasury securities market as the safest most liquid securities market in the world, with maturities stretching from less than 1-mo. to 30-yrs. – the Treasury yield curve functions as the benchmark off which other interest-bearing securities are priced.

Financial services industry professionals use the term spread to define the difference in yield between any fixed income security and the corresponding maturity Treasury security's yield: A spread product[19] is any security that trades at a yield spread to a corresponding maturity Treasury security. The discussions in this chapter and following chapters assumes readers have a basic understanding of fixed income terminology outlined in the Chapter 1.

With approximately $8.5 trillion outstanding, Treasury Agency securities are perceived to be backed by the Full Faith and Credit of the United States Treasury. Agency securities

---

19 Treasury Agencies, Corporate Bonds, Municipals and even Foreign corporate and some Sovereigns.

can be an appropriate holding for risk adverse investors, yet most investors have limited knowledge of agency securities.

Chapter 1 outlined the development of the Treasury securities market via Congressional legislation enacted to finance Depression era programs. After World War-II, civilian infrastructure programs required Congress to enact legislation to create government agencies such as the Federal Farm Credit Bureau, Federal Home Loan Banks (FHLB), Government National Mortgage Association (Ginnie Mae)[20], and government sponsored enterprises Federal National Mortgage Association (Fannie Mae) and Federal Home Loan Mortgage Corporation (Freddie Mac) which are currently operating under conservatorship of the Federal Housing Finance Agency (FHFA)[21] to provide what Congress deemed necessary public services. Treasury agencies are authorized to issue debt; Ginnie Mae, Fannie Mae, and Freddie Mac sell agency backed mortgage pools to investors.

---

20 Ginnie Mae is a division of Housing and Urban Development (HUD) a Federal government agency.
21 FHFA was established September 4th, 2008 and oversees Fannie Mae, Freddie Mac, and the 12 Federal Home Loan banks.

Agency securities have default risk subordinate to Treasury securities and can provide a 200 to 300 basis point spread over the corresponding maturity Treasury security – higher effective yield coupled with vanishingly low default risk. Less than 6% of financial service industry professionals have knowledge of Agency securities, – why most investors are unaware of the benefits of Agency securities.

This chapter discusses the risk / reward characteristics of Collateralized Mortgage Obligations (CMOs)[22] from mortgage pools issued by Ginnie Mae, Fannie Mae, and Freddie Mac. CMOs are complex derivative securities: Investors should consult a financial advisor with an understanding of CMOs before investing.

CMO's are a subset of a larger class of securities known as Mortgage Backed Securities (MBS)[23], the market for which is

---

22 Additional information on CMOs can be found in Appendix 2.

23 Mortgage Backed Securities (MBS) are a subset of securities known as Collateralized Debt Obligations that can be backed by various types of debt i.e. credit card receivables, car loans,

over $5 trillion in size. Mortgage Backed Securities can be collateralized by conventional 30-yr. conforming mortgages or unconventional loans i.e. ARM's[24], Jumbo's, Heloc's, Sub-prime etc... Agency CMOs are only created from conforming[25] collateral pools of Ginnie Mae, Fannie Mae, or Freddie Mac. CMOs issued from Agency collateralized pools of Ginnie Mae (part of HUD) or Fannie Mae and Freddie Mac (FHFA) are backed by the Full Faith and Credit of the U.S. Treasury: other mortgage backed securities (MBS) are not.

CMOs are an engineered product that has been in existence since 1983[26]. Initially investors confused CMOs with Ginnie Mae pass-thru securities issued from the early 1970's which amortized principal over 30-yrs.: CMOs are structured with various principal paydown characteristics. Over the last 35-yrs. of CMO issuance the product has been continually re-engineered to better

---

student loans etc.

24 ARMS; Adjustable Rate Mortgage, occasionally usable as collateral if they had 30-year amortization.

25 In some cases FHA conforming loans along with Fannie Mae and Freddie Mac conforming loans.

26 Salomon Brothers Inc. and First Boston created the first ones for Freddie Mac.

control extension risk[27] early CMOs exhibited during periods of rapidly rising interest rates.

Investors that have purchased homes via conforming[28] mortgages will recall monthly loan payments are part interest and part principal: Conforming mortgages are non-assumable, if the property is sold for any reason (death, divorce, relocation etc.[29]) the mortgage is paid off in full, causing mortgage pools to paydown earlier than the 30-years. All mortgage pool principal payments backing a CMO must be passed on to the CMO holders. Because mortgages can be redeemed at any time, all CMOs have an embedded call option that allows them to be called at any time in entirety.

Interest rates on U.S. issued 30-year conforming mortgages are based on the 10-yr. Treasury note yield, to which mortgage originators add a markup and additional points based on the borrower's credit scores when setting a borrower's mortgage rate. To

---

27 Some CMOs exhibited principal paydown like a 30-yr. pass thru Ginnie Mae.

28 30-yr. fixed rate loan.

29 FHA experience going back to 1934 shows the average mortgage pool pays-off in approximately 7.2 years.

halt ‘70s inflation, the Paul Volcker chaired Federal Reserve raised the Fed Funds rate from 11.2% in late 1979 to a peak of 20% in May 1981, followed by an aggressive 1300 basis point reduction from June 1981 through early 1986: The Fed's actions initially pushed the yield on the 10-yr. Treasury note above 15% and later forced it below 10%, allowing many residential mortgages to be refinanced at lower interest rates. The subsequent refinancing wave caused most CMOs to pay off sooner than anticipated before pre-payment came to a halt in late ’86 when the Federal Reserve once again tightened monetary policy by raising the Fed Funds rate 100 basis points from 6% to 7%.

The 1986 Reagan Administration tax act allowed the financial services industry to create CMOs in a new format known as REMICs’ (Real Estate Mortgage Investment Conduit) that provided for the creation of new varieties of CMO tranches[30] engineered to exhibit specialized principal paydown characteristics. Unfortunately, the '86 tax act went into effect after the Federal Reserve

30 A slice of a mortgage pool collateral.

monetary tightening raised the Fed Funds rate a full 100 basis points from late '86 through early '87 and precipitated a halt in mortgage refinancing that crushed secondary market prices of CMOs.

The October ’87 equity market crash caused the Federal Reserve to abruptly reverse monetary policy to stanch the damage done to the financial markets. The Fed’s quick action reduced the 10-yr. Treasury note yield and jump-started mortgage refinancing that revitalized CMO redemption, but the secondary market price crash left CMOs with a tainted reputation.

The sharp interest rate rise of the late '80s was a learning experience for CMO issuers that forced them to re-engineer the product to better control extension risk: From late '93 through late '94, the newly re-engineered CMO product was subjected to a nearly 200 basis point rise in interest rates when the 10 yr. Treasury note yield went from 5.5% to over 7%, providing CMO issuers an opportunity to observe the products’ maturity extension behavior during an interest rate rise and re-engineer again – a second 200 basis point rise from late '98 through early 2000 caused the 10-yr. Treasury note yield to increase from 4.5% to 6.5%, provided a third opportunity to re-engineer after an interest rate rise.

Currently, CMOs issuance is structured with Planned Amortization tranches (PACs) and companion tranches known as Support tranches engineered to maintain the paydown characteristics of the PACs. Planned Amortization tranches are designed with paydown windows (time-horizons) that provide the PAC tranche a predictable paydown characteristic under various interest rate scenarios. PACs and a variation known as a VADM (very accurately defined maturity) are designed to mimic the bullet-maturity of a standard fixed income security.

The underlying mortgages Agency CMOs are collateralized on is backed by the Full Faith and Credit of the United States Treasury: PACs yield 100 to 200 basis points over the corresponding maturity Treasury security coupled with a predictable principal paydown, making them an attractive investment to a wide range of investors including banks, insurance companies, mutual funds, pension funds, foreign sovereign wealth funds, and even the U.S. Federal Reserve[31].

Support tranches only exist from the creation of PAC tranches: normal mortgage pool amortization[32] would not allow PAC tranches to maintain their planned amortization schedule without a companion tranche to absorb faster rates of principal redemption. The embedded call option in a Support tranche allows it to absorb early return of principal while holding the associated PAC tranche in its' paydown window.

Mortgage collateral securitization currently allows for multiple types of tranches, often multiple PAC tranches are created from a collateral pool. When multiple PACs are created, the front PAC and its associated Support tranches typically take repayment precedent over the others. Front Support CMOs can be the first CMO tranches to pay off in the event of accelerated collateral

---

31 Recall the Federal Reserve's Quantitative Easing Balance Sheet Expansion that included Treasury and Treasury Agency securities.
32 Going back to 1934 the FHA statistics show the average mortgage pool only last 7.2 years.

amortization. Properly engineered Front Supports have been designed to pay-off within 5-years and some Front Supports created since the late '90s have paid off within a 2 to 3-year time horizon. Investors looking for rapid pay down characteristics are advised to carefully research the underlying mortgage collateral before investing in Support tranche CMOs.

Backed by the full faith and credit of the United States Treasury, Support tranche CMO's created from Ginnie Mae, Fannie Mae, or Freddie Mac collateralized mortgage pools can offer investors a 200 to 300 basis point yield spread over the corresponding maturity Treasury security, providing holders monthly interest along with principal payments over a projected time horizon, making them a potential yield enhancement alternative for investors that intend to hold them to maturity.

This discussion simplified the features of a complex derivative security and does not clearly delineate all the risks involved with this complex sector of the fixed income market where investors are best served by employing the knowledge of an experienced financial services professional.

Chapter 3: Corporate Opportunities

The British Government issued consuls[33] as far back as the 18th Century to finance the building of the British Empire. The long-standing existence of British government debt, coupled with Great Britain's high credit rating, made Britain's pound sterling £[34] the reserve currency across the British empire – until World War I, British gilts[35] were the global benchmark for government issued debt. Unfortunately, debt incurred during World War I quickly changed Britain's financial standing in the post-war world, creating confusion in post-war currency and debt markets.

Before the U.S. Treasury debt market evolved from deficit spending caused by the Great Depression and World War II, corporate issued debt was the largest debt sector of U.S. financial markets and railroad bonds[36] were used as a reference for publicly traded debt until early in the 20th Century when the publicly traded debt of

33 Perpetual bonds issued to finance wars.
34 The pound sterling was referred to as coin of the realm.
35 Issued by the Bank of England and originally had a gilded edge hence gilt-edged security.
36 Some railroads issued 100-year "century bond".

American Telephone & Telegraph (AT&T), the world's largest corporation[37], became the benchmark yield curve for U.S. fixed income markets.

Today's investors take for granted the myriad of technological advances over the last 250 years that are viewed as common place today – no one today recalls the digging of the Erie Canal in 1825, the completion of the first transcontinental railroad in 1869, or the construction of telephone landlines: all of which were partially financed by debt.

Security issuance during the 19th Century frequently exposed investors to financial fraud: Today's investors benefit from GAAP accounting standards[38] and regulations imposed by the SEC[39], significant developments 19th Century investors lacked. Technological advances that caused obsolescence of whole industries, also caused the failure of debt securities tied to those business models, the reason most

---

37 Early in the 20th Century AT&T became the largest corporation in the world

38 GAAP; Generally Accepted Accounting Principals

39 Securities & Exchange Commission.

investors deposited their savings in a bank, a strategy that worked if the bank was properly managed.

Throughout the history of the United States, entrepreneurs have created businesses to fill a void. In 1860 Henry Varnum Poor compiled a book of statistical and financial information titled *The History of Railroads and Canals in the United States*. Then in 1868, Poor along with his son Henry William formed a company that began annual publication of a statistical manual titled *Railroads of the United States,* making the Poors the first U.S. providers of third party financial information at a time when most public financing was accomplished by banking institutions utilizing in-house analytical methods.

The increasing volume of securities issuance in the late 19th Century exploited investor interest in the latest technological advances. New industries offering publicly traded securities to satiate investor demand motivated an entrepreneur named Luther Blake in 1906 to fill the information void by founding the Standard Statistical Service[40] to rate the debt of non-railroad companies. Additionally, in 1909, Moody's Investors Service was founded to rate all types of public debt.

Since the early 20th Century, U.S. financial markets have had access to independent ratings for all types of traded securities, but prior to the 1929 stock market crash, investors had no way of knowing if the information issuers provided the ratings services was complete and accurate. The equity market crash and subsequent Great Depression prompted Congress to enact the Securities Act of 1933 and the Securities Exchange Act of 1934[41], which were instrumental in providing standardized accurate financial information (GAAP) for rating services' analysis.

The Securities Exchange Act of '33, requiring public corporations to provide financial information conforming to generally accepted accounting principles (GAAP) was a quantum leap forward for the financial

---

40 Standard Statistical Service and Poors merged in 1941 to become Standard & Poors.

41 The Securities Act of '33 established the U.S. securities regulations and the Securities Exchange Act of '34 established the SEC to enforce the regulations.

markets. Accurate financial information provided the major rating services a clearer view of corporate financials that improved the veracity of their quality rankings and provided investors' confidence when using a security's credit rating to determine if a security's yield spread to the corresponding maturity Treasury security properly compensated for the credit risk.

In 1975 the SEC developed a system to certify ratings services as Nationally Recognized Statistical Rating Organizations (NRSROs)[42] to further assure investors of accurate credit assessment of debt issues. Most investors are familiar with the three largest ratings organizations; Standard & Poors, Moody's, and Fitch Ratings Inc. along with the alphabetical quality ranking scales they provide[43]. The SEC currently certifies ten NRSROs, but not all are certified for securities. The most frequently seen ratings are from the two largest providers: Standard

---

42 The SEC currently certifies 9 organizations as NRSROs; A.M. Best Company Inc., DBRS,Inc., Egan-Jones Ratings Co., Fitch,Inc., HR Ratings De Mexico S.A., Japan Credit Ratings Agency Ltd., Kroll Bond Rating Agency, Moody's Investors Service Inc., Morningstar Credit Ratings LLC, and Standard & Poors Ratings Service.

43 For a complete list of the alphabetical rankings of the four largest ratings services see Appendix 3.

& Poors Financial Services LLC (S&P) and Moody's Investors Service, both of which provide credit rating for all types of fixed income securities – Standard & Poors also rates equity issues and created the S&P 500 Equity Index[44].

Today's fixed income market is more diverse than when Henry Varnum Poor authored his *History of Railroads and Canals in the United State*; public issued debt is no longer composed only of industrials, transports, and utilities; financials, healthcare, food service, and the information age have expanded the variety of industries credit agencies provide ratings on.

Debt issues of similar quality rating don't always trade at the same yield spread to their corresponding Treasury maturity – utility debt typically carries higher yields than similarly rated debt of industrials, financials, or rails. Under varying economic conditions, some segments of the corporate debt market can quickly become overvalued or undervalued – yield spread differences

---

44 The S&P 500 Equity Index is a registered trademark of Standard & Poors Inc., LLC

are the markets' method of accounting for perceived risk differences between issuers. Unpredictable corporate events, such as Union Carbide's December 1984, Bhopal India industrial accident or management malfeasance exhibited by former Tyco International and Health South[45] executives, can drastically impact market sentiment toward an individual issuer, quickly precipitating a dramatic move in the market price of the issuers debt: causing what was an investment grade yield spread to widen to a high yield[46] spread.

Unexpected events[47] that quickly change an issue's credit rating and spread are examples of why investing in corporate debt is a higher maintenance strategy than holding Treasury or Treasury Agency securities.

The preceding discussion illustrated how unexpected corporate events can cause yield spreads to suddenly widen, yet during the last decade of the 20th Century many

---

45 Tyco International's problems surfaced during fiscal 2002 and Health South's in late 2002.
46 High Yield, often referred to as "junk bonds"
47 When a rating change was caused by an LBO take over it was referred to as "event risk".

corporate debt issues narrowed their spread to Treasury securities, making investment grade corporate issues less attractive on a risk adjusted basis. Wall Street's product development wizards were quick to offer a solution to this situation by repackaging corporate debt in the guise of $25 par value, exchange traded preferred issues[48]. The $25 pricing structure made these new preferred issues accessible to small investors searching for higher yields than the bonds they replaced but lacking the default protections of a bond's indenture[49].

Investment in corporate debt requires an understanding of the rating services' credit quality rankings[50] coupled with diligent research. The current pace of global technological advance causes creative destruction that shortens the life of some issuers' business models to less than the maturity of their debt issues, potentially causing dramatic credit rating downgrades.

---

48 Often with colorful names.

49 The legal contract that accompanies all corporate debt issues.

50 Appendix 3 provides the ratings of the 4 largest ratings services.

Exercising diligent investment research may generate higher return from investment grade corporate debt[51] than from Treasury or Treasury Agency securities, but few investors have access to necessary information (accurate pricing[52], ratings changes, call features, indentures etc.) or the experience to consistently select debt issues without the support of an experienced financial services industry professional. Investment grade corporate debt is a sector of the fixed income market where an experienced financial adviser can enhance an investor's chances of success.

---

51 Moody's Baa3 or better and S&P BBB– or better.
52 Bid and Ask

Chapter 4: "Fallen Angels"

During the first eight decades of the 20th Century all new issue corporate debt was investment grade[53] – sub-investment grade[54] debt was a consequence of corporate financial difficulties that caused a corporations' debt rating to fall below investment grade, issues referred to as "fallen angels". In the early 1980s, one of the more prominent fallen angels was Chrysler Corporation. Fortunately, Chrysler chairman Lee Iacocca secured a Federal Government backed loan package allowing Chrysler to develop commercially successful products that provided Chrysler Corporation the funds to pay back the Federal Government guaranteed loans and re-establish an investment grade credit rating.

The 1973 merger of two venerable Wall Street firms, Drexel Firestone and Burnham Lambert to create Drexel Burnham Lambert, provided Mike Milken the venue to create a high yield debt market that reshape investors' opinion of sub-investment grade

---

53 Bond ratings of Moody's Baa3 or S&P BBB– and above.
54 See Appendix 2 for the credit quality ratings attached to sub-investment grade debt.

debt. After acquainting himself with a long forgotten text written by Frederick Macaulay[55] (the father of bond duration[56]), titled *The Movement of Interest Rates, Bond Yields and Stock prices in the United States since 1856*[57] and successfully managing Drexel Burnham's new high yield trading desk, Milken developed new applications for high yield debt, prompting the financial media to crown him the "Junk Bond King".

Frederick Macaulay's book contained a historical study of sub-investment grade debt portfolios vs. investment grade debt portfolios demonstrating the higher coupon yield of sub-investment grade debt more than offset the defaults these portfolios experienced: portfolios composed of high yield debt had a higher total return than portfolios composed of investment grade debt.

---

55 Frederick Macaulay, Aug. 1882 to Mar. 1970 was an institutional economist and author.
56 Two types of duration; Macaulay Duration is a time weighted average until the cash flows from an asset are received measured in years vs. modified duration which is a measurement of a security's sensitivity to interest rate changes, as compounding rate becomes continuous i.e. zero coupon bonds the two duration measurements approach the same value.
57 Originally Published in 1938.

The financial markets didn't initially acknowledge Macaulay's findings and sub-investment grade debt remained an investment back water of Wall Street until the middle '70s when Mike Milken persuaded Drexel Chairman Tubby Burnham to allow him to establish a high yield trading desk at Drexel Burnham.

Milken applied himself with a messianic zeal to develop an in-depth knowledge of all outstanding high yield debt indentures[58] and drove Drexel's new high yield trading desk to profitability within the first year of operation. Importantly, Milken's team was able to cultivate a wide array of high yield debt buyers, some of which eventually became buyers of Milken's innovative use of high yield debt issuance as financing for start-up companies.

New issue sub-investment grade debt, dubbed "junk bonds", suddenly became a cutting-edge product providing needed financing for companies previously excluded from the capital market. The newly

---

58 A bond indenture is the legal document for a debt issue that lays out the bond holders rights to recourse in the event of a default as defined within the indenture.

legitimized form of corporate financing was soon employed to finance corporate mergers and acquisitions – later junk bonds became the preferred financing for leveraged buyouts (LBOs) or extracting "greenmail"[59].

Milken's access to vast amounts of capital provided small LBO partnerships the financial ability to bid for S&P 500 corporations at 1980's fire sale prices: After a successful acquisition, the acquirer would typically proceed to break up the company by selling the pieces for more than the acquisition cost, reaping a quick profit which it could be reinvested in another LBO opportunity. LBO driven corporate restructuring became so prevalent Milken's team hosted an annual soiree in California for Drexel Burnham's high yield clients dubbed the "Predators' Ball"[60].

---

59 LBO firms would buy a large block of stock in a publicly traded company, and then receive a "highly confident" letter from Milken before contacting corporate boards with their LBO offer hoping to entice the targeted board of directors into buying back their stock at a premium to the market.
60 Chronicled in Connie Bruck's; *The Predators' Ball* 1988, Penguin Publishing

The 1980's LBO mania eventually peaked with the 1988, $25 billion buyout of RJR Nabisco by Kohlberg, Kravis & Roberts (KKR)[61]. The financial market media painted RJR Nabisco President and CEO Ross Johnson's behavior during the KKR buyout as the pinnacle executive greed. In the face of KKR's $109/share offer, Johnson made a higher counteroffer of $112/share that reportedly would have netted him a $100 million profit. Under considerable public pressure, RJR Nabisco's board accepted KKR's offer from which Johnson received approximately $60 million before departing the company in early 1989.

The media's portrayal of the RJR Nabisco LBO as all that was wrong with corporate raider restructuring, wasn't the reason for Mike Milken's fall from grace or the 1990 collapse of the high yield market.

During the normal course of business, the SEC reviews financial services firms every three years to verify compliance with all securities regulations. From 1979 onward the regulators had heightened their scrutiny

---

61 Chronicled by Brian Burrough and John Helyar, *Barbarians at the gate; the Fall of RJR Nabisco* 1989, Harper & Row.

of Drexel Burnham and Mike Milken's Beverly Hills, CA high yield trading desk. The SEC dossier on Milken culminated in a ninety-eight-count indictment for racketeering and fraud brought by the SEC against Milken in March of '89.

In April of 1990, Mike Milken pleaded guilty to six counts of securities violation and tax violations: prior to which significant damage to the high yield market had already occurred – on October 13, 1989, the proposed $6.75 billion LBO of UAL Corp.[62] collapsed triggering a price collapse across the high yield bond market.

Milken's plea deal and subsequent prison sentence spelled the end of Drexel Burnham's domination of the high yield market. Eventually the market void was filled by other Wall Street firms, but it took time for the public's perception of high yield bonds to improve.

High yield debt can offer investors yield spreads of 600 to 700 basis points[63] over the

---

62 Then parent company of United Airlines.

corresponding maturity Treasury security. When the 10-yr. Treasury note yielded over 5%, investors could often acquire high yield securities with double digit coupon yields, effectively offering investors equity like returns: inducing some investment professionals to view high yield debt as an equity substitute.

Changing financial market conditions or credit outlook can quickly cause high yield issues to exhibit price volatility: High yield investing is a risk-on strategy. During the 2008 financial market crisis, high yield spreads expanded to 1,500 basis points over corresponding maturity Treasury securities: Bargain prices do not make high yield debt an appropriate investment.

Macaulay's study demonstrated the current yield of sub-investment grade debt mitigated the risk of high yield investing, but today's high yield debt market is noticeably different than the era of fallen angels from which his study was derived.

---

63 The spread is often expressed as 900 basis points over Libor (London Inter-bank Rate).

New issue high yield debt is typically callable in 2 to 5-years at the issuer's discretion: debt restructurings can occur when an issuers' credit rating improves or interest rates drop, impacting the portfolio strategy of high yield funds – maintaining portfolio duration necessitates selling aged holdings approaching a call and replaced it with new longer maturity issues.

High yield issuers depend on the ability to refinance debt. During normal functioning markets, fund managers typically sell the weakest holdings first[64], but investor anxiety precipitated by extreme market conditions can cause redemption driven liquidation of attractive issues. The 2008 financial market crisis was a liquidity collapse that froze high yield issuers access to new capital.

High yield debt liquidation during times of market distress occur at a wider spread to Treasury yields than during normal financial market conditions – late '08 through early '09 was a time investors could buy high yield debt at bargain prices, but many investors overlooked the high yield market due to lack

---

64 Issues with potential credit rating downgrades.

of information. Most high yield issuers don't have publicly traded equity, consequently investors have less access to relevant information – lack of easily available information makes it important investors maintain a relationship with a financial adviser that can provide relevant information on high yield issues.

The high yield sector occasionally provides investment opportunities but owning individual high yield securities has significant risk: Investors should exercise diligence before venturing into the high yield debt.

Chapter 5: Municipal Opportunities

All U.S. residents live within the boundaries of governmental divisions; states, counties, cities, townships, villages – what are referred to as municipalities. Municipalities provide residents with public services such as schools, police & fire departments, libraries, water & sewer services, trash removal etc.; funded by revenues generated from property taxes, sales taxes, license fees etc. – if tax receipts fall short of covering annual operating budgets, municipalities can resort to short term financing – when budgetary shortfalls become a continuing problem or infrastructure improvements are necessary, municipalities can issue long-term debt. This chapter focuses on the $3.7+ trillion municipal debt from more than 90,000[65] issuers.

The original 13 colonies issued debt to finance essential municipal functions: debt obligations known as G.O.s[66], backed by the

---

65 This number assumes the underlying project behind a Conduit bond is counted as the issuer not the municipality which sponsors these issues.

66 General Obligation

taxing authority of the issuing colony. Bridges, turnpikes, or other infrastructure were financed via securities backed by the project's revenues: obligations known as revenue bonds. In the 19th Century municipalities allowed issuance of private entity special purpose debt to finance the building of canals and railroads deemed beneficial to the municipality's economic interests: conduit bonds[67].

After World War II, U.S. cities and states expanded to sizes rivaling foreign country economies: Regardless of size, U.S. municipalities cannot print their own currency[68], yet foreign institutional buyers view U.S. municipal debt as equivalent to sovereign debt – an investment view supported by foreign wealth fund purchases of taxable municipal backed Build America bonds (issued from Feb. 2009 through Dec. 2010[69]) and reinforced in April 2010, when

---

67 The debt was issued via a municipal "wrapper" to help secure a lower financing cost, but the municipality is not responsible for the payment of interest or principal on the debt.
68 The first general circulation paper money by the Federal Government occurred in 1861,"Greenbacks": U.S. Treasury non-interest-bearing demand bills
69 Build America Bonds were legislated by Section 1531 of Title 1 of Division B of the American Recovery and Reinvestment Act signed into law on February 17, 2009.

Moody's Investors Service re-calibrated their U.S. municipal ratings scale to match their global ratings scale[70] – improving transparency of the municipal rating scale for foreign investors. Non-tax-exempt municipal debt, such as Build America bonds, carry higher coupons than corresponding tax-exempt municipal – the combination of higher coupon and low risk profile made Build America bonds an attractive addition to global investors looking to diversify across countries and currencies.

Expanding the municipal investor base improves market liquidity, it doesn't make municipal securities risk free. Experienced investors recall the default of marque municipal names such as New York City in 1975, Cleveland in 1978, Washington Public Power Supply System (WPPSS) in the early '80s, Orange County, CA in Dec. '94, Vallejo, CA in Nov. '08, Jefferson County, AL in 2011, and more recently the July 18, 2013, Detroit, MI, $18 billion Chapter 9[71] filing – the largest

---

70 State and Local G.O ratings moved up by an average of two notches, while State and Local sales and special tax obligations moved up by one notch, enterprise obligations i.e. Revenue bonds did not change.

71 Chapter 9. Title 11 of the United States Bankruptcy Code

filing to date: All the issuers named initially carried investment grade ratings – the $2.25 billion Washington Public Power Supply System, the largest default of the '80s, was initially rated "AAA"[72]. Prior to default, all the debt issues mentioned became fallen angels (high yield debt): Municipalities can experience revenue decline that leads to debt default.

Sovereign debt typically defaults for two reasons: Countries undergoing political upheaval, such as Russia's Bolshevik Revolution and China's Communist Revolution or default on the previous government's debt, while emerging economies typically default via currency[73] devaluation – all of which are a failure of the current government that results in an erosion of the tax base similar to what often occurs with municipality' defaults.

A recent Moody's Investors Service study[74] analyzing municipal defaults from 1970 to

---

available exclusively to municipalities, assists them in restructuring debt.

72 Appendix 5 supplies the four major ratings services alphabetical ratings scales.

73 Currency devaluation is seen as a de-facto default.

74 www.municipalbonds.com/education/read/77/default-rates-

2011, of issues rated by Moody's, found that in any 10-yr. period "A" rated or better municipal issues had a default rate of 0.03%[75]. The same Moody's study emphasized the majority of defaults over the 40-year period (71 in total) primarily occurred in two specific types of revenue bonds: Multi-family Housing and Hospital & Health Service Providers[76], indicating investors can substantially reduce risk by avoiding default prone segments of the municipal market and financially strapped municipalities.

The internet provides investors an abundance of information – access to a security's Cusip #[77] allows investors to view an issuer's Official Statement delineating the purpose of the issue along with the issuer's taxing authority, background information, and pertinent legal information. While the official statement clarifies the bond issue for investors, it typically does not cover the political environment, which can impact the

---

of-municipal-bonds

75 On average 3 defaults for 10,000 issues.

76 Health Service providers includes nursing homes, a type of issue that is often unrated, defaults by unrated issues were not included in the Moody's study that only covered debt rated by Moody's.

77 The Cusip # is the number issued to each security as identification with Depository Trust Co.

issuer’s credit worthiness: Investors should seriously review an issuer's political environment when researching municipal issues.

The discussion of colonial era municipal obligations highlighted three basic types of municipal securities: General Obligation (G.O.s), Revenue, and Conduit bonds. Traditionally, risk adverse municipal investors gravitated to state issued G.O. bonds carrying the full taxing authority of the issuing state. Changing U.S. economic conditions have impacted states’ tax collection and consequently state’ finances. The deterioration of states’ finances due to rising public service employee pension and health care costs has caused several states to have chronic budgetary short falls. State budgetary problems often prompt credit rating agencies to downgrade a state's credit rating which increases borrowing costs and adds to the state's financial problems. Unfortunately, budgetary problems aren’t limited to the state level, many cities and counties have experienced similar difficulties. Most municipalities initially attempt to resolved budgetary problems through tax increases; when the combination of income, property, user, and sales taxes becomes excessive municipalities experience tax base erosion as residents and businesses exhibit tax avoidance behavior or move to lower tax venues. Tax base erosion, as evidenced by migration to the sunbelt, is a growing problem that initially impacted northern industrial cities and states.

During sluggish economic growth and soaring public pension plan deficits, municipal bond investors should seriously evaluate the rationale of investing solely in G.O. bonds – this isn't to imply that G.O. bonds aren’t suitable investments – investors should diligently analyze municipalities potential for downgrades rather than selecting issues simply by name: Investing in municipal securities, by name only, can have disastrous results.

Over the last three decades, municipal investor' interest has gradually shifted toward revenue bonds: municipal debt obligations for which interest and principal payments are dependent on revenues from infrastructure projects financed by the bond issue, not the backing of a municipal taxing authority. Revenue bonds have been issued for airports, bridges, convention centers, parking facilities, schools, sports arenas, toll roads, water & sewer, and gas & electric distribution systems. Revenue bonds such as schools, hospitals, water & sewer, or gas & electric distribution systems are referred to as essential services bonds and are more suitable for risk-averse municipal investors than other types of revenue bonds.

The first decade of the 21st Century, saw innovative revenue bond issues backed by special taxes or assessments such as motor fuel tax, sales tax anticipation bonds, and even tobacco settlements – issues having specific risk factors that can make them unsuitable for risk-adverse investors.

Revenue bonds' higher yield is attractive to investors, but their appeal improved after the 2008 Chapter 9 filing by Vallejo, CA, when a State of California court issued a precedent setting ruling stating revenues collected to pay interest and principal on a revenue bond could not be utilized for purposes other than payment of interest and principal on that specific bond issue. The California court ruling blocking the community of Vallejo, CA's attempt to utilize revenues from their water & sewer system to cover city operating expenses during its' Chapter 9 debt reorganization provided revenue bond issues an implied protection during a Chapter 9 filing. The court instituted change in revenue bond risk profile increased the attractiveness of essential services revenue bonds as an alternative to G.O. issues.

During interest rate declines, investors' reaching for yield, venture into conduit bonds[78] issued to fund private enterprises. Conduit debt is not an obligation of the issuing municipality: Interest and principal payments on conduit debt are an obligation of a private enterprise, not the municipality that provides the municipal wrapper for the financing. Due to the private enterprise aspect of conduit debt, the IRS often classifies interest paid on these issues as AMT[79] income: not fully tax-exempt for all holders.

Investors should view conduit bonds as quasi municipal debt obligations and consult the

---

78 For a further discussion of conduit bonds see Appendix 4.
79 Alternative Minimum Tax Income.

previously mentioned Moody's study findings that issuers such as multifamily housing and hospital & health service providers are the most likely municipal debt to default[80] – much of the non-rated debt (which were not included in the referenced Moody's study) typically carries higher coupons than rated issues are bought by municipal investors familiar with the issue by appealing to the investor's sense of community rather than the investment merits of the issue. The heightened risks of non-rated issues make this sector of the municipal market better suited to mutual funds, closed end funds (CEFs), and UITs: portfolios that can properly diversify.

Conduit bonds' higher coupon yields are accompanied by risk typically associated with high yield corporate debt (junk bonds): Any investment strategy that involves reaching for yield can end badly – high yield municipal debt can be a risky portfolio addition.

---

80 The Moody's study previously mentioned also noted that this type of debt had the lowest cash recovery levels in re-organization.

Discussions of municipal securities requires covering two unique sectors of the municipal bond market: insured issues and issues defeased[81] to maturity with Treasury securities.

The 2008 financial market crisis illustrated why insured municipal issues often carried higher coupon yields than like rated non-insured issues: The higher coupon yield reflected the potential failure of the municipal bond insurance. The '08 crisis caused insurers' portfolio hedges and reinsurance to fail, leaving insurers with liabilities not covered by their assets, some insurers ended up with credit ratings below the underlying credit rating of the municipalities they insured, making the bond insurance worthless. Prior to the 2008 financial market crisis, a hand full of insurance companies offered municipal bond insurance, since the crisis insurers' ranks have been reduced – not surprising since bond defaults typically rise after economic downturns. Fortunately, the 2009 emergence of a mono-line insurer Build America Mutual (BAM), insuring only

81 Referred to as pre-refunded.

qualifying municipal issuers, revitalized the insured segment of the municipal market.

The other unique sector of the municipal market, pre-refunded bonds, remained unaffected by the '08 financial market crisis and continues to provide a tax-exempt income alternative for investors requiring the safety of Treasury securities. The following discussion of municipal defeasance is a simplification of municipal finance intended to explain the basics of pre-refunded issues.

Depending upon the source of funds and the projected payback horizon, municipal financing is typically accomplished by the issuance of serial bonds, callable bonds[82], and term bonds[83] – after paying down the serial issues, municipal issuers with revenue in excess of operating requirements can buy an appropriate amount of Treasury securities to fund an escrow account that covers payment of interest and principal on the remaining debt – the pre-refunding operation transfers the liability from the

---

82 10-yr. call protection

83 Term bonds typically have final maturities two or more years after the issue's serial bond ladder.

municipality's balance sheet to the escrow account. Escrowed municipal debt backed by Treasury securities[84] is seen as having the Full Faith and Credit of the United States Treasury and priced at a small spread to the corresponding maturity Treasury security[85]. Removal of debt from a municipality's balance sheet often results in a credit rating upgrade that reduces municipal borrowing costs – making municipal defeasance a benefit for the municipality and the bond holders.

Municipal securities' unique features: tax-exempt interest and vanishingly low default rates are often overlooked by investors due to misinterpretation of the after-tax effective yield or a lack of understanding of municipal finance.

The after-tax effective yield of an appropriately rated[86] municipal security can be determined through a simple calculation: the tax-exempt coupon is divided by one

---

84 Not all defeasance is accomplished with Treasury securities.
85 To obtain the Treasury credit rating, defeasance is usually accomplished via special issue Treasury SLUGs.
86 Credit quality is an important factor in controlling risk.

minus an investor's marginal tax rate[87] – for an investor in the 38% tax bracket and a municipal security yielding 4% the calculation is as follows; 4.0 / 1 – 0.38 = 6.45% taxable equivalent – an investor in the 38% bracket would need to find a taxable security that yielded better than 6.45% to have a higher after tax effective yield.

Municipal securities, like other sectors of the fixed income market, trade at a yield spread to their corresponding maturity Treasury security, but with an important difference. Most sectors of the fixed income market; Agency securities, corporate, and high yield debt trade at a positive yield spread to the corresponding maturity Treasury security – municipal debt has typically traded at a negative yield spread to the corresponding maturity Treasury security: 30-yr. "Aaa/AAA" municipals typically trade at 90 to 95% of the 30-yr. Treasury yield due to the federal tax-exempt attribute of municipal interest income (the municipal yield spread relationship can change if IRS marginal tax rates change).

---

87 An investor's marginal tax rate is the effective tax rate on the last dollar of income.

During the 2008 financial market crisis Treasury securities exhibited the classic flight to safety (rising prices / falling yields) while other sectors of the fixed income market experienced falling prices / rising yields and a widening of yield spreads. The '08 crisis saw the spread on 30-yr. "Aaa/AAA" rated municipals expand to a positive yield spread of 155% of the 30-yr. Treasury security yield, a situation the municipal market normally doesn't experience. The increase in Chapter 9 filings from early '09 onward delayed the reduction in municipal bond yield spreads providing investors positive tax-exempt yield spreads for a short time.

The discussion up to this point has focused on yield, but credit rating and time horizon are equally important investment parameters. Statistics compiled by the ratings services demonstrate municipal securities have historically exhibited vanishingly low default rates, an important advantage for risk adverse investors, but not a reason for investors to relax their credit parameters by accepting lower credit ratings than they would for corporate debt[88]. Like corporate debt, municipal debt credit ratings can change during economic downturns – violating investment parameters by reaching for yield with lower rated municipal securities can cause loss of capital.

Misconceptions of the effect of local politics on municipal financing causes many investors to overlook municipal bond call features. The discussion on pre-refunding pointed out municipal issuance is often structured with serial bonds, callable bonds, and term bonds that allow issuers to refinance via pre-refunding. Understanding the likelihood of bond calls and pre-refunding is integral to managing a municipal security portfolio. Declining interest rates aren't the only reason municipal debt is called, municipal politics play a larger role in refinancing than many investors realize, cash strapped municipalities will refinance revenue bond issues after most of the serial bonds have matured, extracting cash [89] out the project

---

88 The majority of municipal defaults occur after an economic downturn not during it as in the corporate default cycle.
89 Sometimes the cash is used to balance the budget, other times it is used for other municipal projects.

and deferring debt further out into the future.

The call provision of municipal debt should be utilized when structuring a portfolio. Investors attempting to hold portfolio duration short by purchasing short maturity securities often overlook higher coupon, longer maturity securities that will be called: callable high coupon securities exhibit the duration of short maturity securities coupled with higher current income.

Maximizing portfolio cash flow while maintaining credit rating parameters is of primary importance to most investor but price stability should be equally important. Investors often gravitate to discount or par priced bonds not realizing premium priced cushion bonds[90] provide higher current income and lower price volatility (higher coupon bonds have shorter duration and exhibit less sensitivity to interest rate changes): Premium bond buyers should always calculate yield to worst (YTW[91]).

---

90 Higher coupon premium priced bonds that cushion portfolios against price volatility caused by rising interest rates.
91 Typically the call date.

Tax effective municipal investing requires an after-tax yield equal to or higher than a taxable alternative, often requiring investors to consider longer maturities than they normally would. The yield spread on 15 to 20-yr. callable municipal securities generally offer the best trade-off of after tax effective[92] yield vs. maturity while maintaining credit parameters.

Since the late 1970s, the municipal market has seen a shift from the institutional domination of banks and insurance companies to retail buyers. Professionally managed derivative products such as CEFs, ETFs UITs, and mutual funds compete with private investors' as buyers of individual securities: derivative products hold large sums of capital that requires management to concentrate on large municipal issues[93] which creates opportunities for investors willing to research issues overlooked by fund managers.

---

92 Coupon vs. price.

93 Issues of over $50 million by states, cities, counties, and other well-known issuers.

State's provide local municipalities with approximately 30% of their funding, making it imperative investors consider state credit ratings as part of their investment criteria when researching small municipal issuers. Investors should focus on municipalities in states with investment grade ratings of “Aaa/AAA” through “Aa3/AA-“. Important information such as credit ratings, trade pricing, and official statements (written to clarify all pertinent information relating to the issuer such as financial backing, ratings, size, maturities, bank qualification[94], etc.) can be viewed on the MSRB website[95], providing today's investors an unvarnished picture of the investment suitability of municipal issuers.

The 1986 Federal tax law changes reduced insurance company incentives to buy municipal debt, since that time, professionally managed investment products have had a major influence on the pricing of municipal issues. Investors should thoroughly research state, city, or county issues before investing.

---

94 Bank qualification applies to issues under $10 million.
95 https://emma.msrb.org/

Chapter 6: Preferred Stock

Preferred stock is a hybrid of debt and equity[96] that has existed since the early 19th Century – the earliest preferred stocks were issued as a way of differentiating which shareholders received dividends.

After Federal income tax was established early in the 20th Century[97], the U.S. Congress created various exclusions or "loopholes" to satisfy influential constituents. Currently, IRS tax code allows U.S. corporations to write off interest on debt against earnings before taxes, while dividends are paid out of earnings after taxes[98]: To prevent the double taxation of earnings at the corporate level, Congress created an 85% corporate dividend exclusion for dividends received by corporations holding another corporation's stock. The dividend exclusion provides U.S. corporations the flexibility to raise capital by issuing preferred stock rather than debt or equity. Preferred stocks were initially traded over the counter, with a $100 par value and

---

96 In a corporate liquidation preferred stock is subordinate to debt but ahead of equity.

97 Shortly after the enactment of the Volstead Act that authorized prohibition.

98 Earnings as designated by GAAP accounting standards.

a coupon rate that reflected the 85% corporate tax exclusion, issues that were viewed as institutional preferred.

The early 1990s saw the issuance of variable rate preferred: fixed-to-float, a perpetual security offering a fixed coupon for a set number of years (5, 10, 15 etc.) after which the issuer could redeem the issue or reset the coupon to a predetermined rate[99] and floating-rate securities that periodically reset to a yield spread over short term benchmark (LIBOR[100]) or a specific maturity Treasury yield – these interest rate reset features provide fixed-to-float limited interest rate risk and floating-rate preferred low interest rate risk.

Currently fixed-to-float and floating-rate securities dominate the institutional preferred market: the complexity of these preferred makes it imperative for investors looking to invest develop a relationship with a financial adviser possessing specific knowledge of these securities.

---

99 The rate and reset mechanism are delineated in the offering document (prospectus).
100 LIBOR: the London Inter-bank Offered Rate.

Chapter 3 mentioned the '90s saw the emergence of a new type of exchange traded preferred stock specifically created to attract retail investors: listed preferred issues with a $25 par value[101] that were a recapitalization intended to de-leverage a corporation's balance sheet by refinancing debt as a preferred stock.

The U.S. tax code allows interest paid on debt deductible from earnings ahead of taxes while dividends are not tax deductible, recapitalizing debt with preferred stock potentially has a higher cost of capital for the issuer: the interest carrying cost of debt net of the tax deduction is typically lower than the dividend expense on a preferred issue. Why would a corporation potentially increase its' cost of capital?

All preferred stock, including the new exchange traded variety, has an important difference over debt: Issuers can choose to defer payment of dividends whereas nonpayment of interest on debt would violate debt covenants causing debt holders

---

101 These issues were occasionally tagged with the misnomer baby bonds.

to take legal action. While deferral of a preferred dividend payment[102] is rare and most preferred issues are cumulative (the dividend must eventually be paid), the deferral feature provides an issuer the option to withhold dividend disbursement. Under changed regulatory guidelines the new exchange traded preferred issues had a unique dividend stipulation: financial institutions issuing non-cumulative preferred stock would receive beneficial regulatory treatment.

Most investors are aware U.S. financial institutions operate with borrowed capital (leverage), the cost of capital isn't static, it changes with interest rates, credit ratings, and additionally the Federal Reserve can require an institution hold more Tier-1 capital. Replacing debt with preferred stock allows a financial institution to improve its balance sheet by de-leveraging, potentially decreasing its' cost of capital. After the 2008 financial market crisis, the Fed allowed financial institution issued non-cumulative preferred stock to be counted as Tier 1

---

102 The new preferred issues had a Federal tax clause unknown to most investors that deferred dividends needed to be reported as taxable income, even if the investor hadn't received the dividend (phantom income).

capital: beneficial regulatory treatment is the current reason U.S. financial institutions are the dominate issuers of exchange traded preferred shares.

The new exchange listed preferred stock, like most preferred, are callable perpetuals: Issuers could potentially pay dividends on these securities into perpetuity. Preferred stock, like other fixed income securities, is priced at a yield spread to the corresponding maturity Treasury security. A perpetual preferred has no maturity but its' duration[103] can be approximated and they are typically priced at a yield spread to the 10-year Treasury maturity.

Prior to the 2008 financial crisis preferred stocks traded with approximately a 200-basis point spread to the 10-yr. Treasury yield – during the 2008 financial market crisis, preferred stocks' yield spreads expanded to 1,300 basis points – as the financial crisis receded, preferred spreads hovered around the 400-basis point level (substantially more than "AA" rated

103 The duration of fixed rate exchange traded preferred has been approximated at 6.4 years and fixed- to-float preferred at 6.1 years.

corporate debt) before eventually averaging 300-basis points[104]. All fixed income securities are not equally sensitive to interest rate changes: Treasury securities, corporate debt, and municipal debt are more interest rate sensitive than preferred stock or high yield debt, which tend to be more credit sensitive, investors' opinion of financial institutions' risk changed.

During the '90s, large financial institutions issued preferred stock to improve their balance sheets and benefit from the regulatory treatment of preferred capital – many of these financial institutions underwent severe financial distress during the 2008 financial market crisis requiring a U.S. Government funded bailout. Financial institution bailouts motivated the U.S. Congress to create new regulations prohibiting the concept of too big to fail.[105] In the future, failing financial institutions could be taken over by the Federal Reserve to be liquidated, leaving little value for the shareholders.

---

104 One basis point equals one one-hundredth of one percent.
105 Dodd-Frank Wall Street Reform and the Consumer Protection Act.

The yield spread of an exchange traded preferred vs. the 10-yr. Treasury yield should provide adequate compensation for credit risk. Before investing in fixed-to-float or floating-rate institutional preferred, investors should consult an experienced financial advisor.

Chapter 7: Sovereign Issues

The U.S. Treasury yield curve is the interest rate benchmark for currencies tied to the U.S. dollar, yet many investors didn't realize the 1982 Mexican debt crisis was caused by the Paul Volcker chaired Federal Reserve's unprecedented interest rate actions of the 1980’s.

In 1938, the Mexican government nationalized all foreign and domestic owned oil companies to form *Petr�leos Mexicanos* (Pemex), which became a substantial source of revenue for the Mexican government. Unfortunately, the Mexican government financed Pemex’s exploration and infrastructure via short term debt that required regular auctions of *cetes*[106].

After World War II, major U.S. oil companies[107] proceeded to develop Middle Eastern oil fields. The 1960 formation of the Organization of Petroleum Exporting Countries (OPEC) paved the way for Middle

---

106 Short term Mexican government bills like Treasury bills.
107 Dubbed the Seven Sisters by Enrico Mattei to describe the “Consortium for Iran” that dominated global oil from the mid-1940s to 1970.

Eastern oil producing countries to take control of their destiny – it wasn't until the 1973 Arab Oil boycott that OPEC exerted their control of the oil market prices[108] through embargoes aimed at the U.S. and Israel. OPEC's tactics effectively increased the price of oil and provided the Mexican government the ability to dramatically increase revenues by increasing Pemex's financial leverage as the price of oil rose through the 1970's and early 1980's.

The Mexican peso, like most post World War II currencies[109] was tied to the dollar: debt wasn't a problem while oil prices were rising, and the foreign exchange value of the U.S. dollar was stable. Unfortunately, Paul Volcker's aggressive plan to squash inflation by driving short term[110] U.S. interest rates higher also forced Mexico's short-term borrowing costs to rise. Subjected to rapidly rising interest costs on *cetes*, the Mexican government attempted to resolve its cash crunch by allowing a currency devaluation (technically a debt default) – yield chasing

---

108 Oil is priced in U.S. Dollars the value of which was dropping after the "Nixon shock".
109 The Bretton Woods Agreement.
110 Fed Funds Overnight Rate.

investors that deposited money in Mexican financial institutions experienced a loss of capital.

Mexico's debt problems continued until late '86 when falling oil prices impacted all oil producers[111] precipitating inflation related currency / debt problems across Latin America. The pervasive Latin America debt debacle of the '80s prompted then U.S. Treasury Secretary, Nicholas F. Brady[112] to seek a resolution to Latin Americas' funding problems. In 1988, Brady proposed what became known as the Brady Plan, whereby the U. S. government would help Mexico and Brazil issue U.S. dollar denominated debt, removing currency risk from Latin American debt to facilitate a broadening of their investor base.

Unfortunately, Mexico's currency devaluations didn't end in the '80s. The United States, Canada, and Mexico attempting to improve the cross border economic environment signed the NAFTA[113]

---

111 Continental Bank of Chicago at one time the 7th largest U.S. bank failed in 1984 due to oil field loan defaults.
112 Nicholas F. Brady was U.S. Treasury Secretary from September 15, 1988 to January 17, 1993.
113 NAFTA: the North American Free Trade Agreement,

agreement in December of '92, that went into effect on January 1, 1994. By December of '94, political turmoil and rising debt forced the Mexican government to officially devalue the peso by 15%, an action that emboldened foreign exchange speculators to sell pesos[114]. When the exchange value of the peso finally bottomed, its' value had dropped by 40%, once again destroying investor capital on deposit in Mexican financial institutions.

Mexico wasn't the only emerging market that entangled investors. During the early '90s, emerging market investing came into vogue, Latin America and the newly liberated Eastern European block became popular with emerging market investors and it wasn't long before the Pacific Rim's Asian Tigers[115] were touted as the next big investment opportunity. Investors looking for higher rates of return provided the source of capital to emerging market economies that precipitated rampant

---

114 The selling was typically done via forward futures contracts.

115 Originally Hong Kong, South Korea, Taiwan, Indonesia, Singapore, Thailand, and Malaysia before Hong Kong was absorbed by mainland China.

speculation and fraud on the part of emerging market participants.

Currency induced market distress ensued after Thailand was forced to allow the Thai *bhat* to float freely by cutting its peg to the U.S. dollar in July of '97, to solve its' foreign debt burden. The Thai *bhat* devaluation cascaded across the financial markets of Indonesia, South Korea, Hong Kong, Malaysia, and Laos – even Japan, the world's second largest economy, saw its currency weaken.

The turmoil ended when the IMF stepped in with a $40 billion program to help stabilize the currencies of Thailand, South Korea, and Indonesia but the economic damage was done. Malaysia, as a result of the emerging market currency / debt crisis imposed strict capital controls[116] in January of 1998, that stayed in place until 2005, other countries required almost a decade for economic resolution.

The next currency related financial market shock started on August 8th,1998, when the

---

116 Effectively freezing assets in Malaysia until the crisis controls were lifted in 2005.

Russian government massively devalued the ruble to affect a default on its burgeoning debts, causing a panic in global markets. The ensuing flight to safety was a contributing factor in the collapse of the hedge fund Long-Term Capital Management[117] (LTCM). At times, LTCM had employed 25 to 1 leverage in fixed income convergence trades, merger arbitrage, and hedges on the S&P 500 Index. LTCM lost $4.6 billion within the months of the Ruble Crisis requiring a $3.625 billion bailout from a consortium of banks in late September '98, proving even financial wizards suffer devastating capital losses speculating in non-dollar denominated securities[118].

The attraction of emerging market investing is the potential of higher rates of return than in developed markets, but currency devaluations often obliterate investors' capital.

---

117 The principals of LTCM were the former head of Salomon Brothers Bond Trading, John W. Meriwether and Salomon bond traders along with two future Nobel Laureates; Myron S. Scholes and Robert C. Merton.

118 Roger Lowenstein; *When Genius Failed ; The Rise and Fall of Long-Term Capital Management*, October 9, 2000 Random House publishing

Recent history illustrates emerging market investment is primarily for aggressive risk-oriented investors. Defensive investors seeking diversification from dollar denominated assets should consider debt issues of developed market economies such as the ECU[119] Euro (€), the Japanese Yen (¥), or the British Pound Sterling (£).

Chapter 3's introductory discussion pointed out the Bank of England (BOE) issued debt long before the U.S. Treasury – currently, the Bank of Japan (BOJ) issues debt securities, but the European Union (ECU) Central Bank doesn't, euro (€) denominated debt is typically only issued by corporate entities.

Investors allocating capital to developed markets outside the U.S. will find that foreign sovereign debt typically trades at a negative yield spread to corresponding maturity U.S. Treasury securities[120], making foreign exchange speculation the underlying reason for buying sovereign debt.

---

119 ECU; the European Common Union

120 Recall what the normal yield spread was for municipal securities.

Chapter 8: Fixed Income Strategy Insights

The internet provides an overwhelming quantity of investment advice: it isn't a substitute for investment experience.

This book has deliberately ignored the popular managed investment products of the day[121]; focusing on U.S. Treasury securities, the importance of the U.S. Treasury yield curve as the reference benchmark for pricing of other sectors of the fixed income market and yield spread relationships that provide important insights into risk. Unfortunately, investors seldom utilize U.S. Treasury securities to control portfolio risk and volatility.

U.S. Treasury securities exhibit negative correlation during financial market panics (the flight to safety) – investors often overlook the fact only Treasury securities or cash provide safety and liquidity during financial markets' darkest moments. Investors should establish their risk comfort level and hold an appropriate percentage of

---

121 Mutual Funds, ETFs, UITs, CEFs, etc.

their capital in short-term Treasury securities or cash.

Short-term Treasury securities are a cash substitute that provide income without restricting portfolio liquidity. Investors seeking a higher yield than Treasury securities often allocate capital to riskier assets. The availability of Treasury Agency securities that potentially provide 200 to 300 basis points higher yield than corresponding maturity Treasury securities makes yield chasing foolish.

Treasury Agency MBS securities (CMOs[122]) provide an alternative to
Treasury securities for investors with flexible liquidity requirements. Agency CMOs pay monthly interest and principal but lack a hard maturity date, so interest and monthly principal paydown can vary widely. If investors employ an investment strategy to maximize their effective rate of return CMOs' monthly payments can facilitate a cash management strategy[123] that increases

---

122 Collateralized Mortgage Obligations described in Chapter 4.

123 Paydown can be shorter than the final maturity date: importantly the Full Faith and Credit of the U.S. Treasury implies you will be repaid principal plus interest over the life of

capital faster than lower coupon Treasury securities. Strategies utilizing Agency CMOs are seldom practiced by investors due to a lack of knowledge.

Periods of declining interest rates can make it difficult to maintain income while adhering to appropriate risk parameters – some investors attempting to increase income stray into the high yield sector. High yield debt can potentially exhibit equity like returns, it is a trade, not an investment – never allocate a higher percentage of capital to a high yield security than to an equity position.

Municipal securities provide investors the benefit of tax-exempt income with credit risk second only to U.S. Treasury securities. Investors seeking to reduce their federal tax liability should review their liquidity needs before committing capital to municipal securities.

Investors need to understand their risk comfort level before committing capital – money elicits strong emotions that can cloud

---

the CMO.

one’s judgment, controlling emotions requires knowing one's self. The easiest way to understand one's financial comfort level is to monetize the loss – limit portfolio exposure to an amount that wouldn't violate one’s comfort level.

Appendix 1: Yield Calculations

Interest rates and bond prices are inversely related. When interest rates decline, bond prices rise – conversely, as interest rates rise, bond prices decline. Interest rate change affects current yield and yield to maturity.

The current yield calculation is as follows:

Current Yield = Dollar Amount of Annual Coupon / Current Price, or

Face Value = Dollar Amount of Coupon /Coupon Rate

Dollar Amount of Coupon = Coupon Rate times Face Value

Current yield calculations don't account for the reinvestment value of future cash flows, i.e. interest and principal, for that a yield to maturity calculation is required. Calculated by hand, yield to maturity is a cumbersome reiteration calculation:

Approximate Yield to Maturity = C+ (FV-CP/n) / (FV+CP)/2

C = Coupon express as actual annual dollar amount

FV = Face Value, typically par or $1,000.00

PV= Present Value

N = number of years to maturity

The approximate yield to maturity rate is utilized as (*i*) in the present value calculation to see how close it comes to the market price.

PV = FV / (1 + *i*)n

PV = Present Value i.e. market price

FV = Face Value, typically par or $1,000.00

i = interest rate you are looking for to make the PV calculation = market price

n = number of years to maturity and the number of times (1 +*i*) is multiplied by itself.

If the calculation doesn't equal the bond's current market price, recalculate using a new value for the variable (*i*) until the calculation equals the market price, i.e. the yield to maturity.

Prior to electronic calculators, reiteration calculations were done by hand for increments of one-eighth of a percent to over ten percent across forty-years and published in a book appropriately titled *The Yield Book*. The advent of modern calculators allowed professionals and individuals to quickly calculate yield to maturity for any set of variables. Today, the internet provides websites that allow for accurate yield to maturity calculation.

Investors should understand the yield to maturity calculation and how coupon reinvestment rate impacts total return.

Appendix 2: Understanding Agency CMOs

Chapter 2 discussed Agency securities; specifically, Agency backed CMOs, a misunderstood sector of the Fixed Income markets. The following discussion provides information investors need before deciding if CMOs are a suitable investment.

Safety of Principal

Ginnie Mae is part of HUD[124], the mortgage collateral backing Ginnie Mae CMOs is backed by the Full Faith and Credit of the U.S. Treasury. Fannie Mae & Freddie Mac are currently operated in conservatorship by the FHFA (Federal Housing Finance Agency). Under FHFA conservatorship, Fannie & Freddie mortgage collateral has an implied backing of the U.S. Treasury. With the U.S. Treasury standing behind the timely payment of interest and principal of underlying mortgages, CMO holders will ultimately see a return of principal along with interest. All CMOs have an embedded

---

124 Housing and Urban Development, an Agency of the Federal government.

call option. Buyers of CMOs at par (100) or less cannot lose money if the security is held to maturity, buyers of CMOs at a premium (par+) could experience an early call which reduces the effective yield of the security.

Yield

Agency CMOs typically trade at a positive yield spread to the corresponding maturity Treasury security – CMOs' higher yield is compensation for the uncertainty of final maturity. Mortgage collateral paydown rates can substantially change, impacting the time horizon and the effective yield to CMO holders. Time horizon risk is the main reason for the higher yield CMOs exhibit.

Liquidity

Agency CMOs are self-liquidating securities that pay holders monthly cash flow consisting of interest and principal over the life of the security. Changing mortgage pool principal paydown rates can temporarily halt principal paydown, effectively extending the life of CMOs backed by the pool. While CMOs are trade-able, pricing depends on several factors such as interest rates, mortgage collateral, and paydown speed.

Maturity

CMOs are structured to pay monthly interest and principal: monthly interest payments will be reduced as the mortgage pool principal is reduced. Investors wishing to maintain interest income need to reinvest the returned principal. During rapidly rising interest rates, CMOs exhibit extension risk that causes a sharp reduction in principal payments: mortgage collateral coupon rate is an important factor.

Appendix 3: Credit Ratings

Moody's, Standard & Poors, Fitch, and DBRS are referred to as the big four credit ratings services. All four are certified as a Nationally Recognized Statistical Rating Organization (NRSRO)[125] by the Securities Exchange Commission (SEC). Moody's and Standard & Poors ratings are the two names most investors recognize for fixed income ratings. Listed below are the long-term rating scales for the 4 largest rating services:

Moody's	**S&P**	**Fitch**	**DBRS**[126]
Aaa	AAA	AAA	AAA
Aa1 (high)	AA+	AA+	AA
Aa2	AA	AA	AA
Aa3	AA–	AA–	AA (low)
A1	A+	A+	A (high)
A2	A	A	A
A3	A–	A–	A (low)
Baa1 (high)	BBB+	BBB+	BBB
Baa2	BBB	BBB	BBB
Baa3 (low)	BBB–	BBB–	BBB

---

125 The other firms are A. M. Best Company Inc., Egan-Jones Rating Co., Japan Credit Rating Agency Ltd., Kroll Bond Rating Agency, HR Ratings de Mexico S.A. and Morningstar Credit Ratings LLC.

126 DBRS, founded in 1976 and originally known as Dominion Bond Rating Service is certified a NRSRO.

Ba1	BB+	BB+	BB (high)
Ba2	BB	BB	BB
Ba3	BB–	BB–	BB (low)
B1	B+	B+	B (high)
B2	B	B	B
B3	B–	B–	B (low)
Caa1 (high)	CCC+		CCC
Caa2	CCC	CCC	CCC
Caa3 (low)	CCC-		CCC
			CC (high)
Ca	CC		CC
			CC (low)
C	C		
			DDD
			DD
	D	D	D
NR	NR	NR (Not Rated)	
	R (Regulatory supervision)		
	SD	RD (Selective Default)	
WR (With Drawn)			
U	U (Unsolicited Rating)		

Above the dotted line at Baa3/BBB– is investment grade; below the line is sub-investment grade (High Yield aka Junk Bonds).

Credit ratings are not carved in stone: an issue's ratings can vary over the life of the issue due to changes in the issuer's financial status or technology that changes the dynamics of an industry.

Credit rating agencies typically perform quarterly reviews of corporate finances, occasionally placing individual issuers on positive or negative “credit watch”. An issuer’s credit rating can change at any time – portfolio management a dynamic process.

Appendix 4: Redefining Municipal Bonds

Conduit financing is a politically controversial form of municipal finance. Conduit bonds are revenue bonds issued to fund a private entity deemed to have a "public purpose"; such as hospitals, nursing homes, and low-income public housing developments: projects that are financially questionable as evidenced by the higher occurrence of default highlighted in a Moody's study.[127]

Conduit bond issuance is intended to reduce financing costs of not for profit enterprises that provide necessary services, it is also employed to finance the construction of sports stadiums & exhibition halls: When the financed facilities are privately owned, the bond issue is classified as Alternative Minimum Tax[128] (AMT) and interest is not tax-exempt for all holders.

---

127 http://www.municipalbonds.com/education/read/77/default-rates-of-municipal-bonds

128 AM: Alternative Minimum Tax is a minimum tax imposed on individuals, corporations, trusts, and estates with adjusted income above a threshold amount.

The political logic behind conduit bond issuance is local job creation, it is also an alternative to offering tax breaks or other incentives to sports franchise owners contemplating relocating their franchise. Investors need to understand conduit bonds are typically not an obligation of a municipality.

Some municipalities opt to build and maintain sports facilities leased to sports franchises. If leasing fees fail to cover the municipality's operating costs, the municipality adds these expenses to its yearly operating budget, potentially making municipal owned stadiums a burden to the local taxpayers.

Multi-family low income housing is another questionable use of conduit financing. Section 8, of the Housing Act of 1937, provides government funded housing vouchers for low income individuals. The Federal Governments' definition of low income has been employed by real-estate developers to qualify projects for conduit financing by setting aside a percentage of apartments for a period of twenty-years to residents with incomes sufficiently below an area's median income. After twenty-years, the Section 8 restrictions expire, and the property can be refinanced or sold. Real-estate developers wouldn't undertake a project they didn't expect to be profitable, yet the previously cited Moody's study indicated housing bond issues have a higher default rate, making them inappropriate for investors that prioritize preservation of capital over current income.

The higher coupon yield of conduit bonds can divert investors' attention from comparably rated municipal G.O., or revenue bonds. Conduit bond holders own a security with quasi tax-exempt income[129] that lacks the backing of a municipal taxing authority to cover timely payment of interest and principal. Conduit bonds can be likened to high yield debt (junk bonds): holders of these securities accept business risk for a fixed coupon interest payment. Municipal investors typically don't structure their portfolio to accommodate for the

---

129 Often only partial tax-exemption due to AMT.

defaults that accompany this type of high yield investing.[130]

---

130 Recall the discussion of the underlying principle of high yield investing as laid out in Professor Frederick Macaulay's 1938 book *The Movement of Interest Rates, Bond Yields and Stock Prices in the United States since 1856.*

Appendix 5: REIT Insights

Real Estate Investment Trusts (REITs), are corporations authorized by the Federal REIT Act of 1960 and the Tax Reform Act of 1986 to invest in and operate income producing real estate. The REIT structure allows investors with limited capital access to a professionally managed real estate portfolio.

Equity REITs and real estate management became the 11th industry sector of the S&P 500 Equity Index on September 1, 2016 (mortgage REITs remained in the financial sector).

Investors' gravitate to REITs for their high dividend payout (publicly traded REITS provide an average dividend yield of 3.5 to 4.5%[131]) – IRS regulations require REITs distribute 90% of their taxable operating income.

The following REIT discussion is basic information investors should understand before committing capital.

---

131 REIT yields range from 2% to 8%.

Both private placement (including Reg D.[132]) and SEC registered REITs currently exist. The following discussion covers only public-registered REITs (traded and non-traded) that comply with all SEC regulatory filings.

Public-registered traded and non-traded REITs are created in two basic types: Equity REITs holding rental income properties and Mortgage REITs holding mortgages on income generating properties (a hybrid holding both properties and mortgages[133] occasionally exists). Equity REIT operating income is derived from the rental income. Mortgage REIT operating income is derived from mortgage payments.

The main difference between public-registered traded REITs and public-registered non-traded REITs is liquidity. Investors can buy or sell public-registered traded REITs during market hours, whereas public-registered non-traded REITs typically require a holding period of 7 to 10-years[134] during which investors have limited or no

---

132 Non-registered offerings to fewer than 999 accredited investors and fewer than 35 non-accredited investors.

133 What is referred to as a Hybrid or Combination REIT.

134 A higher dividend yield is provided as enticement for the lack of liquidity.

liquidity. Lack of liquidity is an important reason investment in public-registered non-traded REITs is limited to investors meeting income and net worth requirements (qualified investors). Share pricing is another important difference between public-registered traded and public-registered non-traded REIT. Market transactions determine the share price for public-registered traded REITs, while share price for public-registered non-traded REITs is determined by a third-party independent auditor (FINRA regulations currently require share price audits be accomplished within 29-months of breaking escrow and updated annually[135]): having an independent auditor determined pricing structure of public-registered non-traded REITs makes them a non-correlated asset.

Initially, Equity REITs were the most common REIT format, during the late 1970's Mortgage REITs were created. Mortgage REIT creation was brought to an abrupt halt in the early '80s when the Paul Volcker chaired Federal Reserve sharply raised the Fed Funds rate, forcing U.S. interest rates to

---

135 FINRA Reg. 1502

record levels. Rising interest rates had an outsized impact on leveraged[136] Mortgage REIT portfolios: Operating income was essentially fixed as borrowing costs rose, causing declining mortgage portfolio valuation to decimate their equity.

The high failure rate of Mortgage REITs due to rising interest rates during the late 1970's and 1980's made Mortgage REITs the most failure prone sector of the equity market and cast a pall over all REITs. Given the tarnished reputation of REITs, what attraction beyond their high current dividend yield do REITs hold for income investors.

Public-registered traded and public-registered non-traded Equity REITs exist with dividend yields ranging from 2% to 8%, differences in business models account for the wide range of yields. Income investors attempting to enhance portfolio yield often gravitate to REITs with dividend yields at the high end of the range, a potentially risky strategy in times of rising inflation. Equity REITS typically hold commercial properties

---

136 Many Mortgage REITs borrowed capital to increase their portfolio to make the dividend payout more attractive.

on which they have written long term triple net leases with low lease escalating clauses (often referred to as bond leases), which causes the market pricing of these REITs to exhibit interest rate sensitivity, making them a poor inflation hedge[137].

REIT shares bear all the risks of equity ownership and should not be construed as having the safety of principal associated with investment grade fixed income securities. Investors can utilize REITs as an income producing addition to their equity portfolio, but REITs' holding triple net leases are best seen as a trade, not an investment.

---

137 Income producing real estate is often perceived as an inflation hedge.

About the Author

Mark J. Angioletti has worked as a Registered Rep. in the Financial Services Industry for more than 40 years. Mr. Angioletti holds a Series 7 General Securities License, a Series 63 Uniform Securities License, a Series 53 Municipal Securities Principal License and a Series 65 Registered Investment Advisor License.

The author can be contacted at:
mjangioletti@gmail.com

Made in the USA
Monee, IL
05 November 2026

68020984R00062